DENMARK

UNPACKED

Clive Gifford

WAYLAND
www.waylandbooks.co.uk

First published in Great Britain in 2015 by Wayland
Copyright © Wayland, 2015

Editor: Nicola Edwards
Designer: Peter Clayman
Cover design: Matthew Kelly

Dewey number: 948.9'0612-dc23
ISBN: 978 0 7502 9160 6

Wayland, an imprint of
Hachette Children's Group
Part of Hodder and Stoughton
Carmelite House
50 Victoria Embankment
London EC4Y 0DZ

An Hachette UK Company
www.hachette.co.uk
www.hachettechildrens.co.uk

Printed and bound in China

10 9 8 7 6 5 4 3 2 1

Picture acknowledgements: All images and graphic elements courtesy of
Shutterstock except: p 18 and pp 20-21 (t) Corbis.com.

Contents

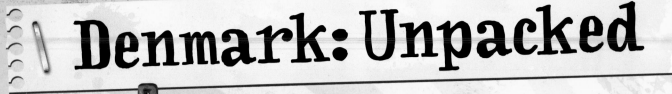

Denmark: Unpacked

So you've come to Denmark. Good on you! You've arrived in a small (just over one-sixth of the size of the UK) yet fascinating northern European nation right in the thick of the action. Denmark has a long and sometimes brutal history as the homeland of many warlike Vikings but it has since become known for much more peaceful endeavours in the arts, science, literature and much, much more. To find out more about the country, the very first amusement park and how a journalist helped out and instantly became an Olympic gold medallist, keep reading!

Fact file

Flag:

Area: 42,916 sq km
Population: 5,627,235
Capital city: Copenhagen
Land borders: Germany
Currency: Danish Krone (DKr)
Main language: Danish

Denmark

Greenland

Kaffeklubben Island

Skagen

Sweden

Denmark

Baltic Sea

Møllehøj

Helsingør

Copenhagen

Zealand

Funen

North Sea

Baltic Sea

Germany

Denmark is made up of the Jutland Peninsula and hundreds of islands. The capital city, Copenhagen, is found on the largest island, Zealand, and is shown here, along with many of the other places you can read about in this book.

At Skagen, the northernmost tip of Denmark, you can walk out onto a sandbar which is washed by waves from two different seas – the North Sea to the west and the Baltic Sea to the east.

You'll find the world's smallest hotel in Denmark... but you'll have to look really hard. It's a one room hotel (the Hotel Central) above a coffee shop in Frederiksberg, Copenhagen.

Lowlands and Islands

Denmark is easily spotted on any map of Europe, jutting out from northern mainland Europe. To the south, it shares its only land border, some 68km long, with Germany, while Sweden and Norway are nearby, across the sea. Sweden is close enough for the 7.84km-long Øresund Bridge and a 4km tunnel to provide a transport link to and from Denmark.

Denmark is home to some 300 species of birds.

Lying Low

Denmark is one of the lowest and flattest countries in the world. Its highest point, Møllehøj, won't test mountain climbers as it is just 170.8m high, and the country's average elevation (height above sea level) is just 31m compared to the UK's 152m, Germany's 263m and Spain's 660m. Denmark's land consists mainly of gently rolling plains, with many lagoons and gulfs which were sculpted by glaciers during the Ice Age. Birdlife is abundant, along with mammals such as hares, hedgehogs and Denmark's biggest wild animal, the red deer.

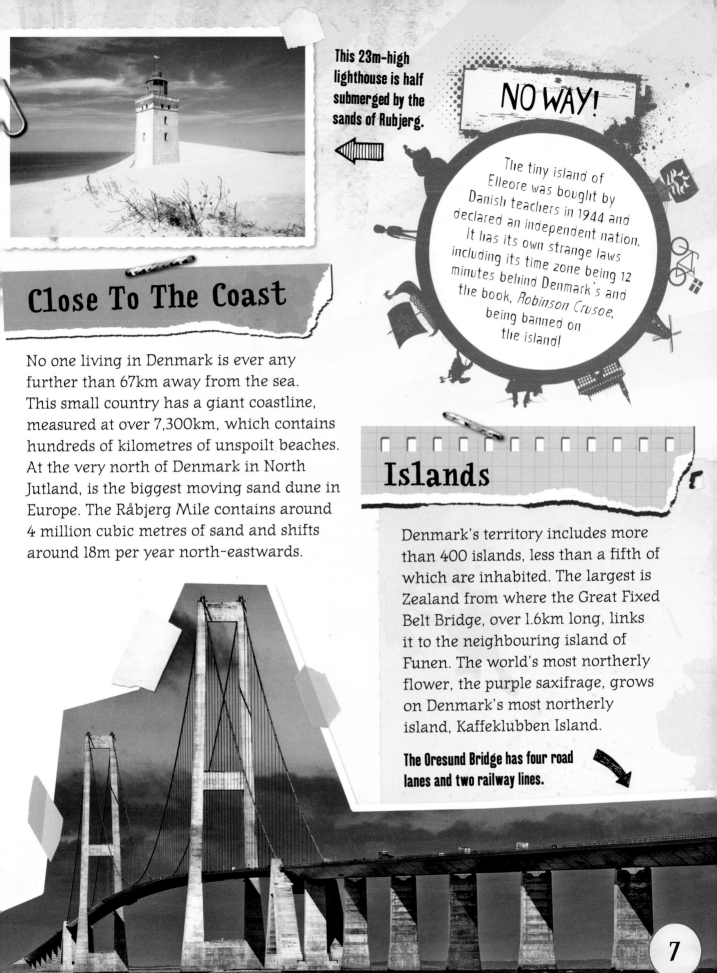

This 23m-high lighthouse is half submerged by the sands of Rubjerg.

Close To The Coast

No one living in Denmark is ever any further than 67km away from the sea. This small country has a giant coastline, measured at over 7,300km, which contains hundreds of kilometres of unspoilt beaches. At the very north of Denmark in North Jutland, is the biggest moving sand dune in Europe. The Råbjerg Mile contains around 4 million cubic metres of sand and shifts around 18m per year north-eastwards.

Islands

Denmark's territory includes more than 400 islands, less than a fifth of which are inhabited. The largest is Zealand from where the Great Fixed Belt Bridge, over 1.6km long, links it to the neighbouring island of Funen. The world's most northerly flower, the purple saxifrage, grows on Denmark's most northerly island, Kaffeklubben Island.

The Oresund Bridge has four road lanes and two railway lines.

Kings, Vikings and Castles

Denmark has been occupied for thousands of years, but took its name from the Danes, a people who colonized the Jutland peninsula in around 500 CE. From the ninth century onwards, Danish Vikings used their formidable seafaring and fighting skills to raid and invade coastal settlements in Europe.

Viking Times

Most Vikings were peaceful stay-at-home farmers but some ranged abroad sailing in knarrs, wide-bodied cargo ships, to trade or narrow, shallow-hulled wooden longships to attack. Five of these ships were discovered in a fjord near the Danish city of Roskilde and now have pride of place in a museum there. The Vikings specialized in hit-and-run attacks on churches and villages on the English and European coast, but over time they began invading and settling parts of England, which became known as the Danelaw. At its peak, it stretched right across England from East Anglia to Cumbria.

An 11th-century ship at the Roskilde Viking Ship Museum.

NO WAY!

Mad King Christian VII (1749-1808), would sometimes greet visiting ambassadors who bowed by playing leapfrog over their backs. As a boy, he roamed the streets of Copenhagen, hitting people with a spiked club.

Denmark's flag flies at Frederick II's castle in Helsingør.

Flagging Victory

King Valdemar II (1170-1241) expanded Denmark's territory into northern Europe, capturing much of northern Germany and Estonia. While he was winning the Battle of Lyndanise in Estonia in 1219, a piece of red cloth marked with a white cross was said to have fallen from the sky. This became the colours of the Dannebrog – Denmark's national flag and one of the oldest national flags in the world.

Royal Fortresses

Between 1574 and 1585, King Frederick II transformed the Kronborg fortress in Helsingør into a spectacular castle, which became the inspiration for Elsinore – the castle in William Shakespeare's play, Hamlet. Frederick II's son, King Christian IV built Rosenborg Castle, which now houses the Danish crown jewels and other finery, including horse saddles encrusted with diamonds, gold and pearls.

Gaining and Losing Territory

Over the centuries, Denmark either formed alliances with Sweden or waged war against its neighbour. From 1397, for example, Sweden, Denmark and Norway formed the Union of Kalmar, with its centre at Copenhagen. In 1536, Norway became part of Denmark and remained linked until 1814, when following defeat in the Napoleonic Wars, Denmark had to give it to Sweden. Iceland, another Danish territory, became independent 130 years later.

Denmark's Royal Life Guards march outside Rosenborg Castle.

Royalty and Rulers

The Danish royal family is one of the longest-running in the world. It can trace back its ancestors not just for a couple of centuries but all the way back to Gorm the Old (who died in 958 CE) and to Harald Bluetooth — considered the first ruler of a united Denmark around 1,000 years ago. That's a lot of history!

All Rise For The Queen

In 2012, Denmark's queen, Margrethe II, celebrated her 40th year on the throne. She was the first female ruler of Denmark since Margrethe I in 1412 and she and her husband, HRH Prince Henrik, are very popular with the Danish people. The Queen speaks five languages and is an accomplished artist who used to exhibit her paintings using a false name, Ingahild Grathmer. She has created illustrations for Danish editions of *The Lord Of The Rings* and has designed dresses and costumes for major movies such as *Wild Swans*!

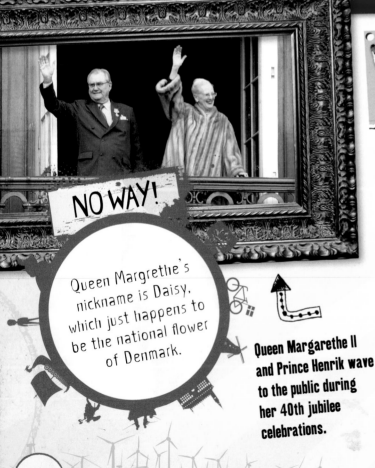

NO WAY!

Queen Margrethe's nickname is Daisy, which just happens to be the national flower of Denmark.

Queen Margarethe II and Prince Henrik wave to the public during her 40th jubilee celebrations.

Palaces and Parties

Amalienborg Palace in Copenhagen is the Danish royal family's traditional winter home, and they spend many autumns and springs at Fredensborg Palace on the banks of Lake Esrum. Members of the royal family make numerous public appearances and host parties and dinners, and Queen Margarethe traditionally gives her Christmas speech to Denmark on New Year's Eve. On occasion, the family travel on the Royal Yacht, named Dannebrog after the country's flag. Since it was first launched in 1931 it has travelled over 650,000km.

The 78m-long Royal Yacht Dannebrog docks in Vordingborg.

In Government

While Queen Margrethe II is head of state, the day-to-day business of running Denmark as a country is carried out by the prime minister, the government of ministers and the Folketing — the Danish parliament, whose 179 elected members sit in Christiansborg Palace. Danes take a keen interest in politics. At Denmark's 2011 General Election, 87.7 per cent of Danes voted, compared to 66.1 per cent in the UK in 2015. The Danes elected the leader of the Social Democrats, Helle Thorning-Schmidt, as their first ever female prime minister.

Christiansborg Palace houses Denmark's law-makers as well as its supreme court.

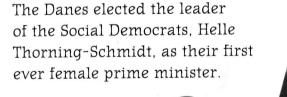

Colourful Copenhagen

Copenhagen is Denmark's capital city and far and away its largest, with over 2 million people living in and around the city. Yet it started out as a humble fishing village more than nine centuries ago. Bishop Absalon built a fortress there in 1167 and afterwards the village took the name Kømandshavn, meaning Merchant's Port.

Ups and Downs

Over the centuries, Copenhagen's wealth and excellent location as a port into the Baltic Sea attracted many attempts to attack it – including by 14th-century German knights, the forces of King Charles X of Sweden and Lord Nelson's British Navy in 1801. The city had a disastrous 18th century. A plague epidemic swept through its flourishing streets in 1711 and killed around a third of the population. This was followed by two major fires, the first starting in a candle shop in 1725 and the second in 1795, which was not helped by firemen being unable to find the keys to the pumphouse (fire station)!

Red tiled roofs and canals dominate this aerial view of Copenhagen.

Warm Welcome

Copenhagen's 4 million visitors each year enjoy a warm welcome from the people and the climate, which is made milder by the warm sea currents. Visitors are drawn to places like the pretty district of Nyhavn, a waterfront district of the city with lots of brightly coloured houses. It is based around a canal dug by Swedish prisoners of war in the 17th century but is now full of attractive wooden ships and cafes on the canal banks. Another tourist haunt is Strøget – a 1.7km-long street area that has been kept free of cars since 1962 and is packed full of shops and cafes.

Nyhavn's scenic waterfront is home to many historic wooden ships.

NO WAY!

A small area of Copenhagen, called Freetown Christiana, is a place containing no cars but around 900 people who try to govern themselves.

Local Landmarks

A well-known meeting place, Kongens Nytorv (King's New Square) is the largest open-air square in Copenhagen. It is bordered by the Royal Theatre, the home of the Danish Royal Ballet. The son of the founder of the Carlsberg brewery was so impressed by a 1909 ballet he saw there that he had a statue commissioned by sculptor Edvard Eriksen, who used the ballerina Ellen Price as a model. The end result, the Little Mermaid statue, now sits on the Copenhagen waterfront at Langelinie Park and is one of Denmark's most photographed landmarks.

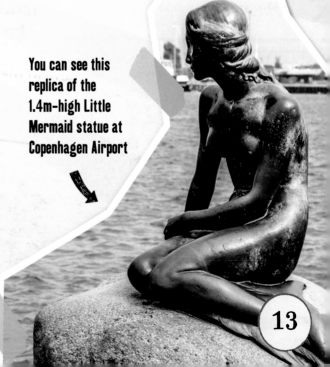

You can see this replica of the 1.4m-high Little Mermaid statue at Copenhagen Airport

Danish Delights

The most famous food connected to Denmark wasn't invented there. The Danish pastry was first baked in the Austrian city of Vienna. But that fact hasn't stopped the Danes adopting the sweet bread treat as a favourite, which they call wienerbrød. Denmark has strict food laws and has banned Marmite, some breakfast cereals and other foods as all of them contained added vitamins. Don't worry, there are plenty of other fascinating foods, so you won't go hungry.

Open sandwiches on rye bread

A golden pretzel hanging over a doorway tells you it's a bakery!

Bake Away

Danish bakeries are busy, busy, busy. The morning meal for most Danes involves rye bread, while lunch is often an open sandwich called smørrebrød. These sandwiches, also made with rye bread, are topped with cold meats, cheese, and spreads. Other common toppings include marinated herring, smoked eel with scrambled egg, pork with red cabbage and prunes! More baking is done to meet the high demand for pastries, biscuits and cakes including *kransekage* (almond cake rings) and *æblekage* (fried apple in breadcrumbs).

Favoured Foods

Like all countries, Denmark has some dishes which seem strange to outsiders although perfectly normal to locals. These include *Hjerter i Flødesovs* (calf's heart stuffed with bacon and served in cream) and *Grilleret lammehoved* (grilled lamb's head). Danes love strong, salty-flavoured liquorice and eat liquorice-flavoured cakes, ice cream, sweets and cakes. They are also big fans of hot dogs bought from street sellers ever since the first hot dog stand appeared in Copenhagen in 1921.

Danish people love hot dogs! Some three million are sold from stands each year.

Built in 1901, the Elephant Gate marks an entrance to the Carlsberg Brewery in Copenhagen.

Beer's Here

Beer has been produced in Denmark for more than 4,000 years and for a small country, Denmark brews an awful lot of beer – over 850 million litres in 2013. Much of it is exported to other countries. The majority of Denmark's beer is made by the Carlsberg brewing company. This brewing giant produces over 500 different types of beer.

Danish Territories

D enmark is a relatively small nation, but when you add its two territories, Greenland and the Faroe Islands, it becomes the 12th largest in the world. While these two territories govern themselves on many matters, they rely on aid from Denmark, their people are Danish citizens and the major currency used is the Danish krone.

Icebergs float in the bay at Illulisat, a town 350km north of the Arctic Circle.

World's Biggest Island

With an area of 2,166,086 sq km, Greenland is the world's biggest island. It's nine times bigger than the UK and almost 50 times larger than Denmark. Around four-fifths of its land is covered in an ice cap. The island's complex 5,800km-long coastline features lots of fjords and small islands, all shaped by glaciers. Greenland's Ilulissat Icefjord is the world's biggest glacier outside of Antarctica. Temperatures on the island are sub-zero for many months of the year, but in summer in central and northern Greenland the Sun remains in the sky from late May to late July.

People of Greenland

The people of Greenland are a mixture of descendants of Inuit, Danish and Norwegian settlers. Almost all of the island's 57,000 inhabitants live on the coast in small settlements. Only five towns, including Nuuk (the capital), Ilulissat and Qaqortoq, hold more than 3,000 people. Greenland has no railways and just 150km of roads. Most transport is by boat, air or using dog sleds. Small-scale farming involves growing root vegetables and tending herds of sheep, goats and reindeer. The Arctic Ocean provides good catches of shrimp, cod and salmon, and fishing and fish processing is the island's main industry.

This catch was made on a frozen fjord near Tasiilaq.

The Faroe Islands

Situated in the North Atlantic Ocean, between Norway, Iceland and Scotland, the Faroe Islands are a cluster of 18 islands separated by deep fjords. Shaped by volcanic activity, these windy islands have sharp cliffs and a thin soil. Trees are sparse, but thick grass provides food for farm animals, mainly sheep, with huge numbers of seabirds along the coastlines. Of the 49,000 or so inhabitants, most work in the fishing industry, with small numbers of people employed in tourism and computing.

This unusual statue of a Faroese Viking is found in the town of Gøta.

A Sporting Nation

For a small country with around a 12th of the UK's population, Denmark has made its mark on the sporting stage. Danish champions include golfer Thomas Bjorn, boxer Mikkel Kessler, nine-time winner of the Le Mans 24-hour endurance motor race Tom Kristensen, tennis star Caroline Wozniacki and Poul-Erik Høyer Larsen — the only player from Europe to win an Olympic gold medal in badminton.

In 2014 and 2015, Christian Eriksen was voted Danish Footballer of the Year.

Soccer Stars

Football is Denmark's favourite sport with over 313,000 registered players and thousands of clubs. The top 12 compete in the Danish Superliga which includes sides such as Brøndby IF, AAB, FC Copenhagen and 2013-14 champions, FC Nordsjælland.

Some of Denmark's best players, including the Laudrup brothers, Michael and Brian, great goalkeeper Peter Schmeichel and Spurs star, Christian Eriksen have won honours playing for clubs abroad. The national team's finest hour came in 1992 when Denmark entered the 1992 European Championships as a last-minute replacement for Yugoslavia, yet went on to win the competition.

NO WAY!

Edgar Aaybe was a Danish journalist reporting on the 1900 Olympics. The Danish-Swedish tug of war team were a man short so they roped in Edgar and went on to beat France in the final, making Edgar the most unlikely Olympic gold medallist ever!

On the Water

As a country with a large coastline, it is no surprise that many Danes enjoy water sports, especially sailing and rowing. In those two sports, Denmark has won a whopping 50 of its 179 Olympic summer games medals, including 19 golds. Denmark's competitive sailors were on top form in 2014 when they won the first ever Sailing Champions League event.

Yachts race at the Danish Open, held at Aarhus.

Handball and Cycling

Handball is another popular sport in Denmark with over 140,000 registered players and great interest in the fortunes of the national men's and women's teams, both of which have won the European Championships. In addition, the women's team have been world and Olympic champions. Denmark has also won 23 Olympic medals in cycling and, in Bjarne Riis, boasts a Tour de France winner. Away from competition, cycling is a hugely popular leisure pursuit in Denmark, with almost 50 per cent of commuters in Copenhagen cycling to work every day.

The Road Racing World Championship was held in Denmark in 2011.

Trade and Power

Denmark joined the European Union at the same time as the UK, in 1973. Today, its biggest trading partners are all in the EU – Germany, the UK and Sweden – with the United States as its largest trading partner outside Europe. Few people (around one per cent) work in agriculture in Denmark. Most work in services with just under a quarter of the working population employed in industry.

Danish Products

Denmark has reserves of oil and natural gas around its coasts, some of which is used as raw materials for its chemicals and pharmaceutical industries. The country exports large amounts of meat, fish and cheese products, as well as furs and manufactured goods such as clothing, electrical items, machinery and furniture. Some internationally famous Danish brands include Pandora for charms and jewellery, Ecco for shoes and TV and electrical goods maker, Bang and Olufsen.

There's plenty to buy in Stroget in Copnhagen, Europe's longest pedestrian shopping area.

The Vestas V164 is the world's biggest wind turbine. Equipped with three 164m-long blades and weighing 1,300 tonnes, a single V164 produces enough electricity in one 24-hour period to power 13,500 Danish homes!

Windy Wonders

More of Denmark's electricity is produced by wind power than any other country in the world. The Danes were pioneers of using wind turbines in the 1970s, and by 2014, 39 per cent of all its electricity was being produced by wind power, with plans for this to rise to 50 per cent by 2020. This has helped spawn a big wind-turbine-making industry, with companies such as Vestas the world leaders. Danish companies have installed over three quarters of all the offshore wind turbines throughout the world!

Denmark's largest offshore wind farm contains 111 wind turbines.

Serious Shipping

Denmark has many ports in which cargo ships and passenger liners can dock. Its largest, the Port of Copenhagen, can handle 40,000 cars at any one time and in 2014, handled over 20 million tonnes of goods and raw materials. In addition, the port caters for cruise ships carrying a whopping 750,000 passengers to the city each year. Denmark is home to the world's biggest container ship operator – the A.P. Møller-Mærsk Group. They operate more than 600 ships including the gigantic Triple E Class vessels which are each 400m long – as long as four football pitches!

A giant container ship moors at Copenhagen's docks.

Design For Life

The Danes take good design seriously, believing that it makes a major difference to people's lives. Danish designers, such as Finn Juhl, Ole Jensen and Hans Wegner, are renowned for the clean, simple and sometimes ingenious lines of their furniture and homewares. Danish design goods, particularly furniture, account for almost 10 per cent of all of the country's exports to other nations.

Architects

Denmark has provided the world with many famous architects. One of the most iconic buildings in the world, Australia's Sydney Opera House, was designed by the Dane, Jørn Utzon who also designed Bagsværd Church and unique housing complexes in and around Copenhagen. Another Copenhagen landmark, the scenic Opera House was designed by Danish architect, Henning Larsen.

Copenhagen's Opera House has 14 floors and seats for up to 1,703 concert goers.

This building was designed by Danish architect Kim Utzon, Jorn Utson's son.

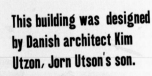

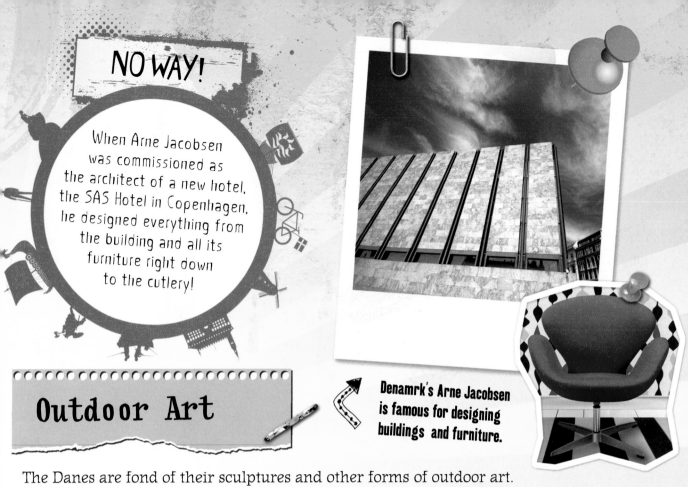

Denamrk's Arne Jacobsen is famous for designing buildings and furniture.

Outdoor Art

The Danes are fond of their sculptures and other forms of outdoor art. One of the biggest in the country is 'Man Meets The Sea', four nine-metre high men made from white concrete that sit close to the town of Esbjerg and stare out to sea. Sculpted in 1995 by Svend Wiig Hansen, these can be seen from up to 10km away. Another fun art installation is the 'Singing Trees of Aalborg'. Musical visitors to Aalborg as varied as Stevie Wonder, Take That and the Vienna Philharmonic Orchestra are asked to plant trees in a park called Kildeparken. Over 70 of these trees have a stand beside them that plays samples of that artist's music when a button is pressed.

'The Man Meets The Sea' statues look out over Sædding Beach in Esbjerg.

That's Entertainment

D anish inventors have given the world's children plenty to play with. KOMPAN, one of the world's leading playground ride makers for example, is based in Denmark. The company was born when Tom Lindhardt Wils, a young Danish artist, saw how children played with sculptures. Here are some more examples of Danish fun and games.

Play Well

Ole Kirk Christiansen was a carpenter from Billund who started building wooden toys first for his sons and then for sale. He set up the Leg Godt – Danish for 'play well' company in 1934. The name was later shortened to LEGO. In the 1950s, LEGO's systems of plastic building bricks started to become popular. Now, they're one of the most played with toys in the world and LEGO's factory at Billund produces around 19 billion bricks and other pieces a year. In 1968, the company opened its first LEGOLAND theme park in Billund. Over 50 million bricks were used to build its exhibits which are viewed by more than 1.6 million people every year.

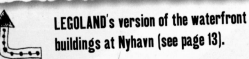

LEGOLAND's version of the waterfront buildings at Nyhavn (see page 13).

Amusing Amusements

In 16th-century Copenhagen, clean fresh water was rare, and the murky local water was known as 'eel soup' – yuk! A Danish lady, Kirsten Piil, discovered a fresh water spring in Dyrehaven Park around 1583 and Dyrehavsbakken, now known as Bakken, became a popular park to gather water, buy from traders and enjoy entertainers. It developed into a big theme park with 33 rides, but is dwarfed by another Copenhagen amusement park, Tivoli Gardens. This picturesque park opened in 1843 and includes one of the oldest wooden rollercoasters still operating in the world.

More than 4.2 million people visited Tivoli Gardens in 2013.

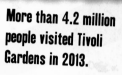

NO WAY!

Born in Denmark, Søren Adam Sørensen was a real practical joker. The jokes he invented included a type of sneezing powder and a toy secret hand buzzer.

A-Mazing Attractions

Visitors flock to Den Blå Planet, Denmark's largest aquarium, in Copenhagen. It has more than 70 giant tanks, one of which contains a massive school of around 3,000 flesh-eating piranhas. Other tanks feature creatures including sharks, stingrays, octopuses and sea otters. Away from Copenhagen, the Natural History Museum in Aarhus contains over 5,000 exhibits of the natural world, while at Samso a giant labyrinth confounds visitors. Constructed from more than 50,000 trees and bushes, it is one of the largest and most complex natural mazes in the world, with 186 choices of routes at different points in the maze.

Den Blå Planet's giant aquarium tanks hold around 7 million litres of water.

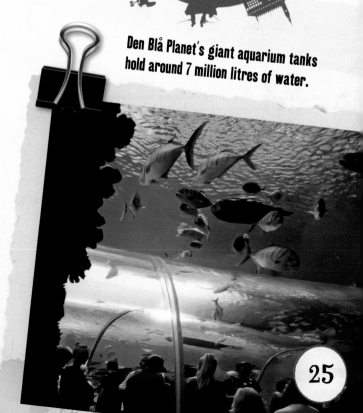

Great Danes

Denmark celebrates many famous Danes who have contributed to the world, from film makers, including Lars von Trier and Gabriel Axel, and famous philosopher Søren Kierkegaard, to explorer Vitus Bering, who in 1728 was the first to sail through the Bering Strait and prove that Asia and North America were separate continents.

Terrific Tycho

Before telescopes were invented, astronomers studied the night sky with the naked eye. A Danish noble, Tycho Brahe (1546-1601), devoted his life to producing the most accurate charts of the night sky ever produced, containing more than 900 stars. Brahe was a colourful character who kept a pet elk in his house and also had a dwarf servant called Jepp. Brahe lost part of his nose in a duel following an argument about a maths equation, but fashioned a false nose out of brass, wax and string!

This statue of Tycho Brahe stands near Rosenborg Castle in Copenhagen.

Master Storyteller

Hans Christian Andersen was dyslexic and was never able to spell well when he wrote his now world-famous stories for children. International Children's Book Day is celebrated on his birthday – the 2nd of April.

Born in the Danish city of Odense, Hans Christian Andersen (1805-1875) travelled to Copenhagen to work as an actor. There, he began writing novels, plays and stories for children, the first collection of the latter, *Fairy Tales, Told for Children*, being published in 1835. More followed. His fairy stories featured humour, sadness and memorable characters. Many of these tales, including The Ugly Duckling, The Little Mermaid, Thumbelina and The Princess and the Pea, are read to this day.

Prize Guys

Danes have won some 13 Nobel Prizes, in literature, medicine and the sciences. Niels Bohr won the 1922 Nobel Prize for Physics for explaining the structure of atoms and 53 years later, his son, Aage, won the same prize, also for work on atoms. In 1903 a scientist from the Faroe Islands, Niels Ryberg Finsen, became a Nobel Prize winner for his work on how to treat diseases including Lupus.

 A bronze statue of Hans Christian Andersen, located next to Copenhagen's City Hall.

A Happy People

International surveys of the lives of people in different countries produced by the European Union, the United Nations and other organizations regularly place Denmark at or near the top. The country's people are thought of as some of the happiest in the world. What is their secret? Is it Denmark's mild climate or is it something else?

Copenhagen University founded in 1479, is Denmark's oldest, and boasts an impressive library.

Money Matters

Denmark is a wealthy country. Its people enjoy some of the highest wages in Europe but also pay some of the highest taxes, including 25 per cent VAT on goods. In return, the state provides high levels of education, health care and support for families. Parents of a new baby, for example, get 52 weeks of paid holiday between them – the joint highest in Europe. Almost all further education at universities and colleges is not only free, but Danish students are paid a monthly sum called Statens Uddannelsesstøtte to help them live.

Families enjoy an outdoor children's theatre performance.

NO WAY!

One of Denmark's odd laws is about personal names. Parents can only choose from a list of 7,000 approved first names. In addition, nearly a quarter of all Danes have the surname Jensen, Nielsen or Hansen.

Out and About

Denmark's picturesque countryside, coast and islands encourage its people to get out and about. Vast numbers cycle, walk and swim regularly, which may have something to do with Denmark being ranked as one of the healthiest countries in Europe. Yet more attend the many festivals and events put on around the country. Many Danes feel strongly about their community and help out when they can. Around 40 per cent of all Danish people volunteer for charities or unpaid activities.

Hygge!

Danes are punctual, tend to speak their mind and don't give empty compliments, but that doesn't mean they don't love to meet up and socialize. In fact, they have a special word for it – *hygge* – which means feeling cosy and snug as you enjoy other people's company. *Hygge* often involves inviting people into others' homes in the evening, shutting out the troubles or the cold. The greatest compliment you can pay your hosts is to thank them for a cosy evening.

Hygge can even apply in summer, when Danes meet friends and family outside at markets or as here, at one of the country's smokehouses.

More Information

Websites

http://denmark.dk/en
Visit the official website of Denmark, which is full of information about the country and its people.

http://www.visitdenmark.co.uk/en-gb/denmark/vikings
Check out this great website, which has lots of interesting information on the Vikings in Denmark.

http://www.copenhagen.com
Learn more about Denmark's capital city at its official website.

http://www.recordholders.org/en/list/lego.html
See the world's biggest LEGO tower and other record breakers at this website.

http://kongehuset.dk/english/front-page
The official homepage of the Danish Royal Family.

Apps

Triposo Denmark Travel Guide
A handy guide to the cities and key tourist sites of Denmark.

Learn Danish 6000 Words
Learn to speak commonly used Danish words and phrases using this ace app which helps you test your knowledge with a series of small games.

1001 Stories of Denmark
A fact-packed app full of details about large numbers of different sights and attractions from all over Denmark.

Movies

Otto is A Rhino Award-winning animated movie in which a boy with a great imagination draws a rhino which comes to life.

Pelle The Conqueror This dramatic movie about a father and son from Sweden who move to live in Denmark won numerous awards.

Max Pinling Also known as Max Embarrassing, this movie tells the tale of a boy who has what he thinks is the world's most embarrassing mother.

Clips

https://www.youtube.com/watch?v=MpirbD3UoEc&list=PL149F0DF0561A50C1
Sneak some peeks at the beautiful Frederiksborg Castle

https://www.youtube.com/watch?v=A4baGQg_OFw
Become a passenger on the Demon Ride rollercoaster at Tivoli Gardens in this great point of view video.

https://www.youtube.com/watch?v=ghtiZ-t4G4i
Take a scenic trip around southwest Greenland and its biggest settlement – the city of Qaqortoq in this seven-minute mini documentary.

Books

Denmark (Major European Nations) – Heather Docalavich and Shaina Indovino (Mason Crest Publishers, 2013)

Denmark (Cultures of the World) – Robert Pateman (Cavendish Square Publishing, 2006)

The Complete Fairy Tales – Hans Christian Andersen (Canterbury Classics, 2014)

The Best and Worst Jobs in Anglo-Saxon and Viking Times – Clive Gifford (Wayland, 2015)

From 1448 onwards, all the kings of Denmark were either named Frederick or Christian with one exception – King Hans (1455-1513).

Glossary

elected – To be selected or picked for a job by people voting.

epidemic – When an infectious disease spreads across a wide area or among a large number of people at a particular time.

exports – Goods or raw materials that are sent to another country for sale or trade.

fjord – A long narrow inlet from the sea.

fortress – A large building or group of buildings used as a stronghold by an army or other military force.

glacier – Large, slowly moving mass of ice.

lagoon – An area of shallow water separated from the sea by sand dunes.

manufacturing industry – Businesses that turn raw materials into finished parts or goods for sale.

marinated – Describes food such as fish or meat that has been soaked in a flavourful liquid.

peninsula – A piece of land that juts out from the rest of the land and is largely surrounded by water.

pharmaceutical industry – The industry concerned with producing medical drugs.

picturesque – A place that is particularly pretty or scenic.

tonne – A unit of weight equal to 1,000kg.

VAT – Short for valued added tax, it is a form of tax placed on goods that are bought.

Vikings – Seafaring pirates and traders from Scandinavia who invaded and settled coastal areas of Europe in the 8th-11th centuries.

Index

Unpacked

Australia
Australia: Unpacked
Exploration and Discovery
City Sights
Not All Desert
Aussie Animals
Long Distance Travellers
Go, Aussie, Go!
Mine Time
On the Coast
Native Australians
Aussie Tucker
Everyday Life
Coming to Australia

978 0 7502 8424 0

Brazil
Brazil: Unpacked
A World of Faces
Let's Go to Rio!
Viva Futebol!
Jungle Giant
Nature's Treasure Trove
Highways and Skyways
Bright Lights, Big Cities
Life, Brazilian Style
Looking Good
Arts for All
Adventurous Tastes
Prepare to Party!

978 0 7502 8402 8

China
China: Unpacked
The Story of China
One in a Billion
Futuristic Cities
A World in One
Country Life
Going Places
Ancient Arts
Made in China
Be a Sport
Land of the Panda
Believe it!
Let's Eat Together

978 0 7502 9172 9

Croatia
Croatia: Unpacked
Kaleidoscope Country
Pay a Visit
Sea and Snow
Time-Travel Cities
Country Quiet
Playing Ball
In the Wild
Being Croatian
A Place in Europe
All You Can Eat
Festival Fun
Creative Croatia

978 0 7502 9163 7

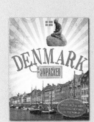

Denmark
Denmark: Unpacked
Lowlands and Islands
Kings, Vikings and Castles
Royalty and Rulers
Colourful Copenhagen
Danish Delights
Danish Territories
A Sporting Nation
Trade and Power
Design for Life
That's Entertainment
Great Danes
A Happy People

978 0 7502 9160 6

France
France: Unpacked
The City of Light
Ruling France
Fruit of the Earth
Home and Away
Power and Progress
Grand Designs
Bon Appetit
The Arts
En Vacance
Made in France
Allez Sport
Life in France

978 0 7502 8416 5

Germany
Germany: Unpacked
Forests, Rivers and Lakes
East and West
Dinner Time!
Energy and Ecology
Knights and Castles
Football Crazy!
Super Cities
Big Brains
Great Days Out
The Car's the Star
Quirky Germany
All the Arts

978 0 7502 9166 8

India
India: Unpacked
From 0 to a Billion
Touring India
Everyone's Game
Wild Wonders
Rocks, Rivers, Rains
Life on the Land
High-tech, Low-tech!
Staggering Cities
Everyday India
Spice is Nice
Bollywood Beats
Bright Arts

978 0 7502 8417 2

Italy
Italy: Unpacked
The Romans
Rome: the Eternal City
Way to Go
Food Glorious Food
La Bella Figura
Mountains and Volcanoes
The Italian Arts
Calcio!
North and South
Everyday Life
Super Cities
Italian Inventions

978 0 7502 8401 1

Mexico
Mexico: Unpacked
Viva Mexico!
Land of Extremes
City Living
Wonders of the World
Working the Land
It's a Winner
On the Move
Going Wild
Lively Life
On the Money
Ready to Eat?
Amazing Arts

978 0 7502 9169 9

Poland
Poland: Unpacked
Wondrous Warsaw
The Land
Super Scientists
Food for Thought
Work and School
Sport in Poland
Great Gdańsk
Religion and Tradition
The Poles at Play
Art and Music
Fabulous Festivals
Uniquely Polish

978 0 7502 9157 6

Portugal
Portugal: Unpacked
Small Country, Big Story
Let's Play!
Holiday Hotspot
Sun, Sand and Serras
Island Magic
Charismatic Cities
Made in Portugal!
Country Corkers
Wild Times
Make Yourself at Home
Surf 'n Turf
Creative Culture

978 0 7502 8843 9

South Africa
South Africa: Unpacked
Three Capitals
The Land
Becoming South Africa
SA Sport
Farming
Rainbow Nation
Fabulous Food
Rich and Poor
Wild Life
Mineral Wealth
On the Coast
Holidays and Festivals

978 0 7502 8844 6

Spain
Spain: Unpacked
A World of Their Own
Fiesta Forever
On the Ball
Highlands and Islands
Sleepless Cities
Escape to the Country
Wild Spain
Spanish Life
All You Can Eat
Hola World!
Olé, Olé!
Eye-Popping Arts

978 0 7502 8425 7